Naturalization Research Records:

A Family Tree Research Workbook

By Catherine Coulter

Naturalization Research Records: A Family Tree Research Workbook
Copyright © 2013 Catherine Coulter
All rights reserved
ISBN-13: 978-1484970263
ISBN-10: 1484970268

Books Written By Catherine Coulter

My Family Tree Research Records

Family Group Research Records

Census Research Records

Cemetery and Funeral Home Research Records

Court House Research Records

Web Log and Web Accounts

Naturalization Research Records

Military Research Records

Immigration Research Records

My Family Tree Notebook

Internet Addresses and Accounts

Books Written by Catherine Coulter under the name of Cathy Coulter

The Man in Red

A Children's Book of Poems Goodnight and Hello

The decision to emigrate was not an easy decision to make. Our ancestor's faced many obstacles in order to do so, such as gaining enough money, the many steps they had to go through just to get aboard a ship, and the dangers involved with emigration. There were many reasons why our ancestor's emigrated as well, several of the main reasons for doing so were political and religious freedoms, a better life, and to get away from conflicts or famine. But, for whatever the reason they chose to do so they faced many ordeals on the way and overcame them to start their new lives in their new country.

Whether they came by sail boat, steamship or entered America through Ellis Island, Castle Garden or some other port, our ancestors came here to settle into a new life and raise their families. Apart of that new life for some meant becoming citizens. In order to do so they had to go through the naturalization process that took years to accomplish. In doing so, our ancestors left us a record trail to follow in our search of them.

The naturalization records can be a bit tricky to find them all. A person coming to America wanting to become naturalized had several steps to go through before it became finalized. The naturalization process changed over time and depending on the year you are searching you will need to be aware of the rules. There were a minimum number of years an immigrant had to have been in America and a minimum number of years they had to have lived in the state where they wanted to start the process before they could. Then after the intent to become naturalized had been filed there was another wait until they could file naturalization papers. During this time period they could move to another state and file the final naturalization papers there. They also had to have references from someone who was already a citizen.

Now citizenship for children and the wives were in connection with that of the husband/father for some time. The fact that a child born in America did not always mean that they were considered as being a citizen upon birth, even if the parents were not. That came into law eventually but keep in mind it was not always so. If a child was under a certain age when their father became a citizen then they too gained citizenship. If not then they had to go through the process as well if they were to be considered a citizen.

If you know the date of naturalization or approximant year you can search the internet for the requirements for citizenship for that time period. It helps knowing this information because it could very well tell you what year your ancestor immigrated and just how long he resided in a particular state and where to look for the records.

If you have the year they arrived in America and not the date of naturalization You can research the naturalization laws of that time to get an idea of when they may have applied for naturalization. This will give you a clue as to where to search for the naturalization records.

The Naturalization Research Log will help you at the court house when searching for the naturalization records. It will help keep track of those you have found and those you still want to look for. It also will help you keep track of which county and state you have looked in for your ancestors. Once, competed it will also Help you find the naturalization information you have discovered and filled in on the worksheets in this book. I have included a section as well for the recording of naturalization information that could be found on a Naturalization Petition

Getting a photo copy of the record often comes in handy and saves time at the court house. If for some reason you can't get a photo copy of the record you may be allowed to take a photo of it. This way if any questions come up on the notes you took you will not have to go back to the court house again to look at it again.

Naturalization Research Log

Ancestor's Name	State	County	Found	Page #

Naturalization Research Records

County of _____ State of _____

Location of Record Found_____

_____

If you already know this information this will help confirm that you have the right record. If not then you will be able to fill it in as you find the records.

Full Name	
Date of Birth		Place of Birth	
Occupation	

Current Residence at time of petition_____

Wife's Name		Birthdate	
Child's Name		Birthdate	
Child's Name		Birthdate	
Child's Name		Birthdate	
Child's Name		Birthdate	
Child's Name		Birthdate	
Child's Name		Birthdate	

Date of Petition	District Court	Emigration Date	Emigrated From	Date of Emigration

Port of Arrival	Date of Arrival	Name of Vessel

Witnesses_____

_____

_____

Notes:

Naturalization Research Records

County of _____ State of_____

Location of Record Found_____

_____

If you already know this information this will help confirm that you have the right record. If not then you will be able to fill it in as you find the records.

Full Name	
Date of Birth	Place of Birth
Occupation	

Current Residence at time of petition_____

Wife's Name		Birthdate	
Child's Name		Birthdate	
Child's Name		Birthdate	
Child's Name		Birthdate	
Child's Name		Birthdate	
Child's Name		Birthdate	
Child's Name		Birthdate	

Date of Petition	District Court	Emigration Date	Emigrated From	Date of Emigration

Port of Arrival	Date of Arrival	Name of Vessel

Witnesses_____

_____

Notes:

Naturalization Research Records

County of _____ State of_____

Location of Record Found_____

_____

If you already know this information this will help confirm that you have the right record. If not then you will be able to fill it in as you find the records.

Full Name	
Date of Birth	Place of Birth
Occupation	

Current Residence at time of petition_____

Wife's Name		Birthdate	
Child's Name		Birthdate	
Child's Name		Birthdate	
Child's Name		Birthdate	
Child's Name		Birthdate	
Child's Name		Birthdate	
Child's Name		Birthdate	

Date of Petition	District Court	Emigration Date	Emigrated From	Date of Emigration

Port of Arrival	Date of Arrival	Name of Vessel

Witnesses_____

_____

_____

Notes:

Naturalization Research Records

County of _____ State of_____

Location of Record Found_____

_____

If you already know this information this will help confirm that you have the right record. If not then you will be able to fill it in as you find the records.

Full Name	
Date of Birth	Place of Birth
Occupation	

Current Residence at time of petition_____

Wife's Name		Birthdate	
Child's Name		Birthdate	
Child's Name		Birthdate	
Child's Name		Birthdate	
Child's Name		Birthdate	
Child's Name		Birthdate	
Child's Name		Birthdate	

Date of Petition	District Court	Emigration Date	Emigrated From	Date of Emigration

Port of Arrival	Date of Arrival	Name of Vessel

Witnesses_____

_____

_____

Notes:

Naturalization Research Records

County of _____ State of_____

Location of Record Found_____

_____

If you already know this information this will help confirm that you have the right record. If not then you will be able to fill it in as you find the records.

Full Name	
Date of Birth		Place of Birth	
Occupation	

Current Residence at time of petition_____

Wife's Name		Birthdate	
Child's Name		Birthdate	
Child's Name		Birthdate	
Child's Name		Birthdate	
Child's Name		Birthdate	
Child's Name		Birthdate	
Child's Name		Birthdate	

Date of Petition	District Court	Emigration Date	Emigrated From	Date of Emigration

Port of Arrival	Date of Arrival	Name of Vessel

Witnesses_____

_____

_____

Notes:

Naturalization Research Records

County of _____ State of_____

Location of Record Found_____

_____

If you already know this information this will help confirm that you have the right record. If not then you will be able to fill it in as you find the records.

Full Name	
Date of Birth	Place of Birth
Occupation	

Current Residence at time of petition_____

Wife's Name		Birthdate	
Child's Name		Birthdate	
Child's Name		Birthdate	
Child's Name		Birthdate	
Child's Name		Birthdate	
Child's Name		Birthdate	
Child's Name		Birthdate	

Date of Petition	District Court	Emigration Date	Emigrated From	Date of Emigration

Port of Arrival	Date of Arrival	Name of Vessel

Witnesses_____

_____

Notes:

Naturalization Research Records

County of _____ State of_____

Location of Record Found_____

_____

If you already know this information this will help confirm that you have the right record. If not then you will be able to fill it in as you find the records.

Full Name	
Date of Birth	Place of Birth
Occupation	

Current Residence at time of petition_____

Wife's Name		Birthdate	
Child's Name		Birthdate	
Child's Name		Birthdate	
Child's Name		Birthdate	
Child's Name		Birthdate	
Child's Name		Birthdate	
Child's Name		Birthdate	

Date of Petition	District Court	Emigration Date	Emigrated From	Date of Emigration

Port of Arrival	Date of Arrival	Name of Vessel

Witnesses_____

_____

_____

Notes:

Naturalization Research Records

County of _____ State of_____

Location of Record Found_____

_____

If you already know this information this will help confirm that you have the right record. If not then you will be able to fill it in as you find the records.

Full Name	
Date of Birth	Place of Birth
Occupation	

Current Residence at time of petition_____

Wife's Name		Birthdate	
Child's Name		Birthdate	
Child's Name		Birthdate	
Child's Name		Birthdate	
Child's Name		Birthdate	
Child's Name		Birthdate	
Child's Name		Birthdate	

Date of Petition	District Court	Emigration Date	Emigrated From	Date of Emigration

Port of Arrival	Date of Arrival	Name of Vessel

Witnesses_____

_____

_____

Notes:

Naturalization Research Records

County of _____ State of_____
Location of Record Found_____

_____

If you already know this information this will help confirm that you have the right record. If not then you will be able to fill it in as you find the records.

Full Name	
Date of Birth	Place of Birth
Occupation	

Current Residence at time of petition_____

Wife's Name		Birthdate	
Child's Name		Birthdate	
Child's Name		Birthdate	
Child's Name		Birthdate	
Child's Name		Birthdate	
Child's Name		Birthdate	
Child's Name		Birthdate	

Date of Petition	District Court	Emigration Date	Emigrated From	Date of Emigration

Port of Arrival	Date of Arrival	Name of Vessel

Witnesses_____

_____

_____

Notes:

Naturalization Research Records

County of _____ State of_____

Location of Record Found_____

_____

If you already know this information this will help confirm that you have the right record. If not then you will be able to fill it in as you find the records.

Full Name	
Date of Birth	Place of Birth
Occupation	

Current Residence at time of petition_____

Wife's Name		Birthdate	
Child's Name		Birthdate	
Child's Name		Birthdate	
Child's Name		Birthdate	
Child's Name		Birthdate	
Child's Name		Birthdate	
Child's Name		Birthdate	

Date of Petition	District Court	Emigration Date	Emigrated From	Date of Emigration

Port of Arrival	Date of Arrival	Name of Vessel

Witnesses_____

_____

_____

Notes:

Naturalization Research Records

County of _____ State of_____

Location of Record Found_____

_____

If you already know this information this will help confirm that you have the right record. If not then you will be able to fill it in as you find the records.

Full Name	
Date of Birth		Place of Birth	
Occupation	

Current Residence at time of petition_____

Wife's Name		Birthdate	
Child's Name		Birthdate	
Child's Name		Birthdate	
Child's Name		Birthdate	
Child's Name		Birthdate	
Child's Name		Birthdate	
Child's Name		Birthdate	

Date of Petition	District Court	Emigration Date	Emigrated From	Date of Emigration

Port of Arrival	Date of Arrival	Name of Vessel

Witnesses_____

_____

_____

Notes:

Naturalization Research Records

County of _____ State of_____

Location of Record Found_____

_____

If you already know this information this will help confirm that you have the right record. If not then you will be able to fill it in as you find the records.

Full Name	
Date of Birth	Place of Birth
Occupation	

Current Residence at time of petition_____

Wife's Name		Birthdate	
Child's Name		Birthdate	
Child's Name		Birthdate	
Child's Name		Birthdate	
Child's Name		Birthdate	
Child's Name		Birthdate	
Child's Name		Birthdate	

Date of Petition	District Court	Emigration Date	Emigrated From	Date of Emigration

Port of Arrival	Date of Arrival	Name of Vessel

Witnesses_____

_____

_____

Notes:

Naturalization Research Records

County of _____ State of_____

Location of Record Found_____

_____

If you already know this information this will help confirm that you have the right record. If not then you will be able to fill it in as you find the records.

Full Name	
Date of Birth	Place of Birth
Occupation	

Current Residence at time of petition_____

Wife's Name		Birthdate	
Child's Name		Birthdate	
Child's Name		Birthdate	
Child's Name		Birthdate	
Child's Name		Birthdate	
Child's Name		Birthdate	
Child's Name		Birthdate	

Date of Petition	District Court	Emigration Date	Emigrated From	Date of Emigration

Port of Arrival	Date of Arrival	Name of Vessel

Witnesses_____

_____

_____

Notes:

Naturalization Research Records

County of _____ State of _____

Location of Record Found _____

_____

If you already know this information this will help confirm that you have the right record. If not then you will be able to fill it in as you find the records.

Full Name	
Date of Birth	Place of Birth
Occupation	

Current Residence at time of petition _____

Wife's Name		Birthdate	
Child's Name		Birthdate	
Child's Name		Birthdate	
Child's Name		Birthdate	
Child's Name		Birthdate	
Child's Name		Birthdate	
Child's Name		Birthdate	

Date of Petition	District Court	Emigration Date	Emigrated From	Date of Emigration

Port of Arrival	Date of Arrival	Name of Vessel

Witnesses _____

_____

Notes:

Naturalization Research Records

County of _____ State of_____

Location of Record Found_____

_____

If you already know this information this will help confirm that you have the right record. If not then you will be able to fill it in as you find the records.

Full Name	
Date of Birth	Place of Birth
Occupation	

Current Residence at time of petition_____

Wife's Name		Birthdate	
Child's Name		Birthdate	
Child's Name		Birthdate	
Child's Name		Birthdate	
Child's Name		Birthdate	
Child's Name		Birthdate	
Child's Name		Birthdate	

Date of Petition	District Court	Emigration Date	Emigrated From	Date of Emigration

Port of Arrival	Date of Arrival	Name of Vessel

Witnesses_____

_____

_____

Notes:

Naturalization Research Records

County of _____ State of_____

Location of Record Found_____

_____

If you already know this information this will help confirm that you have the right record. If not then you will be able to fill it in as you find the records.

Full Name	
Date of Birth	Place of Birth
Occupation	

Current Residence at time of petition_____

Wife's Name		Birthdate	
Child's Name		Birthdate	
Child's Name		Birthdate	
Child's Name		Birthdate	
Child's Name		Birthdate	
Child's Name		Birthdate	
Child's Name		Birthdate	

Date of Petition	District Court	Emigration Date	Emigrated From	Date of Emigration

Port of Arrival	Date of Arrival	Name of Vessel

Witnesses_____

_____

_____

Notes:

Naturalization Research Records

County of _____ State of_____

Location of Record Found_____

_____

If you already know this information this will help confirm that you have the right record. If not then you will be able to fill it in as you find the records.

Full Name	
Date of Birth	Place of Birth
Occupation	

Current Residence at time of petition_____

Wife's Name		Birthdate	
Child's Name		Birthdate	
Child's Name		Birthdate	
Child's Name		Birthdate	
Child's Name		Birthdate	
Child's Name		Birthdate	
Child's Name		Birthdate	

Date of Petition	District Court	Emigration Date	Emigrated From	Date of Emigration

Port of Arrival	Date of Arrival	Name of Vessel

Witnesses_____

_____

_____

Notes:

Naturalization Research Records

County of _____ State of_____

Location of Record Found_____

_____

If you already know this information this will help confirm that you have the right record. If not then you will be able to fill it in as you find the records.

Full Name	
Date of Birth	Place of Birth
Occupation	

Current Residence at time of petition_____

Wife's Name		Birthdate	
Child's Name		Birthdate	
Child's Name		Birthdate	
Child's Name		Birthdate	
Child's Name		Birthdate	
Child's Name		Birthdate	
Child's Name		Birthdate	

Date of Petition	District Court	Emigration Date	Emigrated From	Date of Emigration

Port of Arrival	Date of Arrival	Name of Vessel

Witnesses_____

_____

Notes:

Naturalization Research Records

County of _____ State of _____
Location of Record Found _____
_____

If you already know this information this will help confirm that you have the right record. If not then you will be able to fill it in as you find the records.

Full Name	
Date of Birth	Place of Birth
Occupation	

Current Residence at time of petition _____

Wife's Name		Birthdate	
Child's Name		Birthdate	
Child's Name		Birthdate	
Child's Name		Birthdate	
Child's Name		Birthdate	
Child's Name		Birthdate	
Child's Name		Birthdate	

Date of Petition	District Court	Emigration Date	Emigrated From	Date of Emigration

Port of Arrival	Date of Arrival	Name of Vessel

Witnesses _____
_____
_____

Notes:

Naturalization Research Records

County of _____ State of_____

Location of Record Found_____

_____

If you already know this information this will help confirm that you have the right record. If not then you will be able to fill it in as you find the records.

Full Name	
Date of Birth	Place of Birth
Occupation	

Current Residence at time of petition_____

Wife's Name		Birthdate	
Child's Name		Birthdate	
Child's Name		Birthdate	
Child's Name		Birthdate	
Child's Name		Birthdate	
Child's Name		Birthdate	
Child's Name		Birthdate	

Date of Petition	District Court	Emigration Date	Emigrated From	Date of Emigration

Port of Arrival	Date of Arrival	Name of Vessel

Witnesses_____

_____

_____

Notes:

Naturalization Research Records

County of _____ State of_____

Location of Record Found_____

_____

If you already know this information this will help confirm that you have the right record. If not then you will be able to fill it in as you find the records.

Full Name	
Date of Birth	Place of Birth
Occupation	

Current Residence at time of petition_____

Wife's Name		Birthdate	
Child's Name		Birthdate	
Child's Name		Birthdate	
Child's Name		Birthdate	
Child's Name		Birthdate	
Child's Name		Birthdate	
Child's Name		Birthdate	

Date of Petition	District Court	Emigration Date	Emigrated From	Date of Emigration

Port of Arrival	Date of Arrival	Name of Vessel

Witnesses_____

_____

_____

Notes:

Naturalization Research Records

County of _____ State of _____

Location of Record Found_____

_____

If you already know this information this will help confirm that you have the right record. If not then you will be able to fill it in as you find the records.

Full Name	
Date of Birth	Place of Birth
Occupation	

Current Residence at time of petition_____

Wife's Name		Birthdate	
Child's Name		Birthdate	
Child's Name		Birthdate	
Child's Name		Birthdate	
Child's Name		Birthdate	
Child's Name		Birthdate	
Child's Name		Birthdate	

Date of Petition	District Court	Emigration Date	Emigrated From	Date of Emigration

Port of Arrival	Date of Arrival	Name of Vessel

Witnesses_____

_____

Notes:

Naturalization Research Records

County of _____ State of_____

Location of Record Found_____

_____

If you already know this information this will help confirm that you have the right record. If not then you will be able to fill it in as you find the records.

Full Name	
Date of Birth		Place of Birth	
Occupation	

Current Residence at time of petition_____

Wife's Name		Birthdate	
Child's Name		Birthdate	
Child's Name		Birthdate	
Child's Name		Birthdate	
Child's Name		Birthdate	
Child's Name		Birthdate	
Child's Name		Birthdate	

Date of Petition	District Court	Emigration Date	Emigrated From	Date of Emigration

Port of Arrival	Date of Arrival	Name of Vessel

Witnesses_____

_____

_____

Notes:

Naturalization Research Records

County of _____ State of_____

Location of Record Found_____

_____

If you already know this information this will help confirm that you have the right record. If not then you will be able to fill it in as you find the records.

Full Name	
Date of Birth		Place of Birth	
Occupation	

Current Residence at time of petition_____

Wife's Name		Birthdate	
Child's Name		Birthdate	
Child's Name		Birthdate	
Child's Name		Birthdate	
Child's Name		Birthdate	
Child's Name		Birthdate	
Child's Name		Birthdate	

Date of Petition	District Court	Emigration Date	Emigrated From	Date of Emigration

Port of Arrival	Date of Arrival	Name of Vessel

Witnesses_____

_____

_____

Notes:

www.ingramcontent.com/pod-product-compliance
Lightning Source LLC
Chambersburg PA
CBHW080759290526
45790CB00008B/3520